CUSTOMER SERVICE:
AIMING FOR EXCELLENCE

"Everything you were expected to know about Customer Service, but no one ever told you!" ©

Timothy P. Bonomo

Concepts in Communications
in association with
Trafford Publishing/Canada

Illustrations/Photos by Karen M. Bonomo
Edited by Karla Bonomo Verdi

Contact the author, send in your stories, or share your comments.
E-mail Tim at *AimforExcellence@aol.com*

National Library of Canada Cataloguing in Publication

Bonomo, Timothy P., 1960-
    Customer service : aiming for excellence / Timothy P. Bonomo.

ISBN 1-55369-542-9
    1. Customer services. I. Title.

HF5415.5.B65 2002   658.8'12   C2002-
902119-7

TRAFFORD

This book was published *on-demand* in cooperation with Trafford Publishing.
On-demand publishing is a unique process and service of making a book available for retail sale to the public taking advantage of on-demand manufacturing and Internet marketing.
On-demand publishing includes promotions, retail sales, manufacturing, order fulfilment, accounting and collecting royalties on behalf of the author.

Suite 6E, 2333 Government St., Victoria, B.C. V8T 4P4, CANADA

Phone	250-383-6864	Toll-free	1-888-232-4444 (Canada & US)
Fax	250-383-6804	E-mail	sales@trafford.com
Web site	www.trafford.com	TRAFFORD PUBLISHING IS A DIVISION OF TRAFFORD HOLDINGS LTD.	
Trafford Catalogue #02-0355		www.trafford.com/robots/02-0355.html	

10   9   8   7   6   5   4   3

Dedication

To my special friends and supporters whose efforts on my behalf are more important than I can express.

To my sisters, Karla and Karen, for their faith, encouragement and their impressive talents without which this book would not have been possible.

To my father, Bob, who illustrated true strength of character and an iron will, tempered with compassion; who recently passed away after a courageous struggle with cancer.

To my children, Nicholas and Kelly, by far my greatest accomplishments.

And finally to my wife, Doreen, for her support, understanding, and tolerance of all my "great projects".

Contents

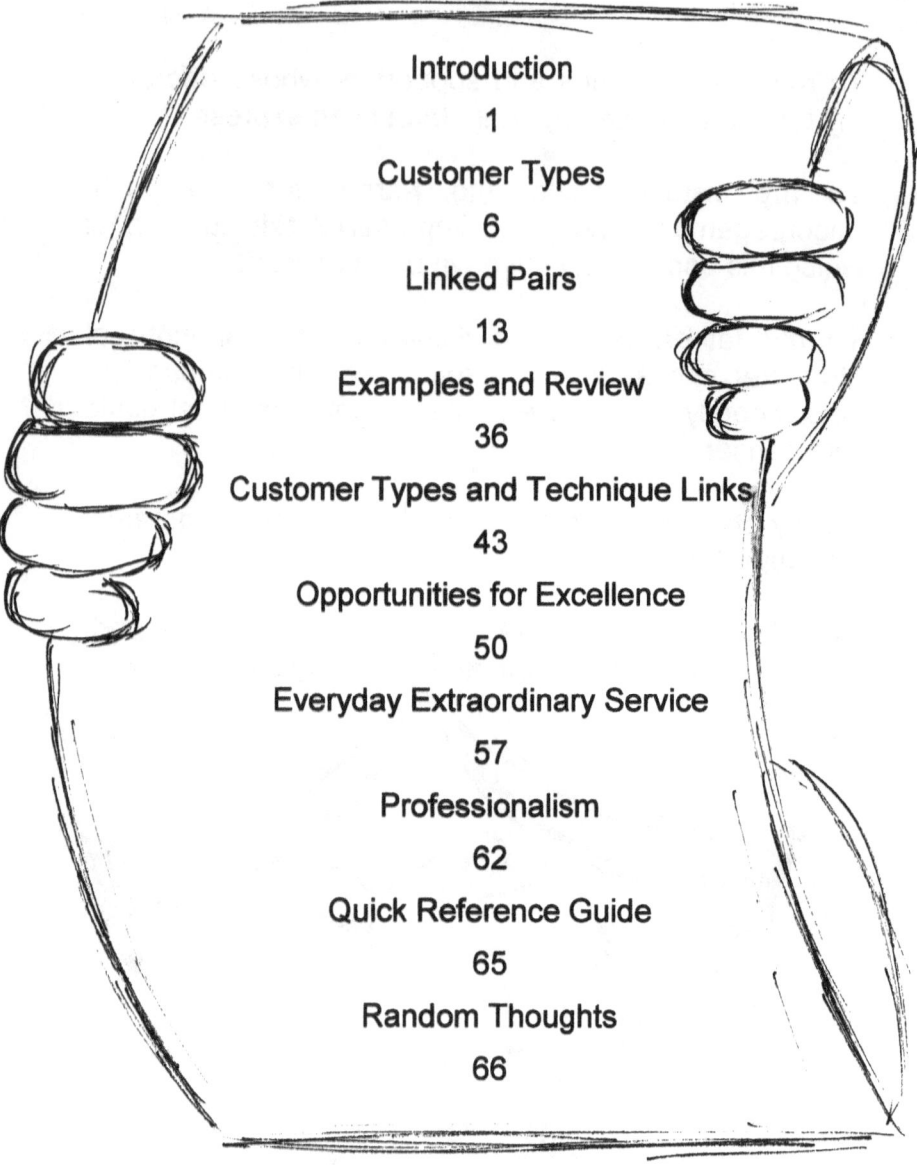

Forward

When I began this project I knew that Customer Service was considered.... "a concern", "an opportunity for improvement", "a challenge area".... Oh heck, lets face it; **it's a problem**! A lot has happened since then, I have given speeches, conducted classes and, perhaps most importantly, I have had the wonderful opportunity to engage in many discussions about why Customer Service is in crisis and what can be done to help.

One of the venues for these discussions is a class that I teach for the Business Development Center of a local college. In this class, I get a great variety of business people, students, managers and front line employees. They all have something to say about customers and providing customer service. I usually open the class by telling them about a story that I heard while I was in college. Let me share it with you...

The professor told us about a group of managers in a large manufacturing facility that had, in an attempt to increase productivity, begun to brainstorm one day about how to motivate their line workers. After much discussion, the management group decided that they would try to increase production by installing higher wattage bulbs. The logic was that if the employees could see better they would naturally work faster and more efficiently.

Dozens of man-hours were devoted to the project and after considerable time and expense the entire production line was re-lamped. Soon after, measurements were taken to determine the effect that the brighter bulbs had made on productivity.

The results were impressive and productivity went up substantially. Bolstered by their success (and no doubt by the thought of promotions and raises soon to come) the management team planned a massive effort to re-lamp the entire plant.

There was even talk about proposing this on a company-wide scale. There was one young executive; however, who remained a little skeptical. Although he couldn't argue with the proven statistics he did question whether the increased brightness of the bulbs was the *actual* cause of the improvement.   Being quite persuasive, he finally convinced his associates to allow him to test, what seemed to be, the obvious results. They took a smaller section of the line, in a different part of the plant, and decreased the wattage of the bulbs. The instructor asked us what we thought had happened. Well, logic seemed to dictate that productivity would go down. Right? Guess what? Productivity actually went up! That revelation made everyone sit back and re-think the assumptions that they had been making.

After some additional experimentation and fact-finding a conclusion was finally drawn. The conclusion was that the lighting had little to do with the increase in productivity, and that in fact, the real reason for the improvement was that the employees felt that management was concerned about them and their work environment. The employees had discussed all of this at length and the feeling of being paid attention to coupled with their increased awareness of their own productivity levels were the real motivators.

One of the reasons that I tell this story is to illustrate the concept that anyone who reads this book (or goes through the seminar) ***will be*** better at Customer Service.

Just as the line workers in the factory, the fact that you are spending time learning about customer service will undoubtedly increase your awareness and therefore your skills.

I like to tell the people in my class that "this is not rocket science" but that statement can be a little misleading. Although much of what I present simply makes sense (and thankfully requires none of those mind-numbing calculations) it is in some ways even more difficult.

With the given laws of physics and the material world it is very possible to predict a reaction to virtually every action. When human beings are involved, however, there aren't many hard, fast rules and when two humans interact…anything can happen.

In this book you will find some "patterns", some "trends", some generally applicable rules but remember to apply them with the soul of an artist (as opposed to the rigidity of a scientist). After you have learned these techniques and listened to my observations combine them with your own experiences and your own personality to create an even more sophisticated way to provide excellence in Customer Service.

That is what this book is all about…. beginning the dialog, initiating the thought processes and considering new perspectives.

I hope you enjoy the ride.

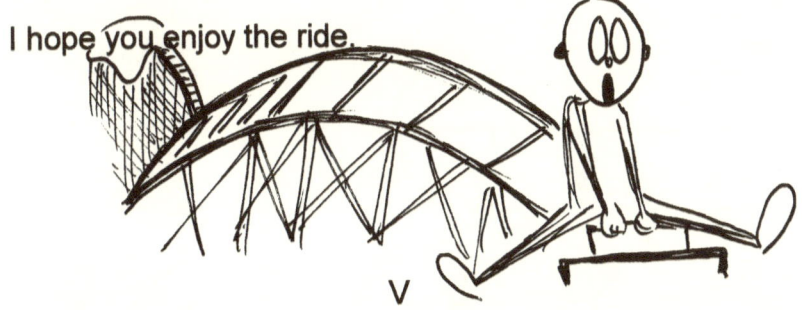

v

Introduction

There isn't a company out there that doesn't claim to have customer service as one of their highest priorities. That's wonderful but what do they do about it? Is there training involved? Do they offer seminars, books or other tools to develop and sharpen customer service skills?

Honestly? Not very often.

It is both a shame and very puzzling to me. We spend billions of dollars on training programs annually and yet the "piece-of-the-pie" allotted to customer service is actually quite small. Why would any company spend hours and hours teaching new employees how to:

- ✓ use a computer program
- ✓ ring out a cash register
- ✓ build a component
- ✓ learn a process or
- ✓ make a burger

Then, drop the ball on Customer Service? Especially since, Customer Service, alone, is the one thing that will transcend and impact absolutely everything that their employee will ever do!

My opinion is that this is because of what I call the *"Assumption of Competency Phenomenon"*. Less enlightened organizations assume that since we all experience customer service dozens of times daily, we *must* already know how to do it correctly. Fuzzy thinking like that is precisely what creates the crisis of customer service we are facing today.

1

The truth is *IF* we were lucky enough to experience *excellent* customer service multiple time's daily then, yes, there would be a chance that we might pick up some of the skills. Let's use an analogy to explore this *"Assumption of Competency Phenomenon"* further.

Suppose that I go to buy a pizza from *the best* pizza maker in town, everyday, for a month. While I am there I watch him very carefully, kneading the dough, stretching it, hand tossing it, finishing it with toppings and then cooking it. Now, if I tried to do the same thing alone, without any help or instruction. Well, let's just say that I wouldn't want to eat the results and neither would you!

And remember I was watching the best pizza maker in town!

To continue the analogy... what if I had been watching one of the worst pizza makers in town? The really disturbing part is that if I was suddenly thrust into a situation where I had to make a pizza by myself I would still, most likely, try to copy him. You have to remember that even though he was one of the worst pizza makers in town he still knew more about it than me! If you apply the same type of warped thinking evident in the *"Assumption of Competency Phenomenon"* I should be able to make a pizza quite well after simply having seen it done, but ask yourself... Could you make a high quality pizza given the same set of circumstances?

Most of the customer service we experience daily is, quite frankly, horrendous. Is that what we should model? I don't think so. But that is exactly what happens.

2

The good news is that there are some organizations that claim customer service is a high priority and then actually does something to ensure it.

By the way…congratulations…You care!

What a huge step in the right direction! The fact that you are reading this book speaks volumes about your commitment and automatically sets you apart from 90% of the organizations and employees out there today.

Okay, so either you have an interest in Customer Service yourself or you have been told about this book by someone, most likely someone from work.

The only real reason you should be reading this is that giving excellent customer service is important to you. There is an old saying that goes like this.

"A man convinced against his will, is a man of the same opinion still."

Obviously having someone trying to force you to provide excellent customer service is simply not going to work. If, however, you recognize how much *more fun* being at work can be when things "go right", then you are ready to learn some very practical ways to make that happen more often.

Let's answer one question right up front.

Is giving excellent customer service realistic?

YES! ABSOLUTELY!

A very important distinction needs to be made from the start, however. *Excellent* customer service is not *perfect* customer service. I don't know about you, but I haven't seen anything that is "perfect" yet. So, I am not shooting for perfection, but I am... *Aiming for Excellence.*

One thing you will notice as you read this book is that there is an honesty about it. That is no accident. I was not interested in writing a book that was purely academic. I think of this as more of a "survival guide". A survival handbook needs to be realistic and easily understood or you could die! Now, while providing bad customer service might not kill you, providing poor customer service *can* make you wish you were dead.

In any case, since we are going to be spending a little time together, let me make some promises to you from the start.

I will try to...
- ✓ make this as painless as possible, maybe even a little fun.
- ✓ be as realistic as possible. We will discuss customer service as it occurs in the "real world", honestly.
- ✓ keep this as short as possible. You probably have other things you would like to be doing and I will not waste your time.

Great, now that I have made these promises to you. It is time for you to make a commitment to me. *Hey, remember that I said I would keep this discussion "real".* No one gives you something for nothing, so since I have anted up my part, now it's your turn! Here are the 3 simple things that I would ask of you.

4

You will try to…

✓ <u>consider the suggestions that I make</u>. Not all of them necessarily, but the ideas that seem to make sense to you, personally.

✓ <u>agree to try at least 1 of the techniques that I will offer</u>. If not, don't waste your time reading this. Go do something fun and come back when you are ready.

✓ <u>share your insights and thoughts about this book with at least 1 other person</u>. Good, bad, it doesn't matter, but you do have to talk about it with someone else.

That's it! No, really. No hidden clauses, no more to buy, no salesman will call, no club to join. Pretty simple huh? Well that's the whole point of this book, simple ideas, simply put.

Okay! Now that we are done with the preliminaries lets jump into this topic!

Customer Types

"The good, the bad and the ugly"

I certainly would not be keeping my promise about honesty if I didn't talk realistically about the many, many types of customers we have all had to deal with at one time or another.

Hey, one important point, I almost forgot *"Customers" should be defined as anyone you work for or with.* So, that means, they can be external (from outside of your organization) or internal (people who work for the same company that you do).

In developing the customer types for this book. I looked at the most often encountered types of customers and then grouped them into categories. As I started to describe each of these types I found myself using adjectives/traits that seemed to be describing certain types of animals instead of customers. That's when the customer types were born.

Let me show you how this worked out, here are some of the adjectives/descriptors I was using to describe one customer type.

Industrious, busy, determined, always on the move, goal oriented, fast-paced, focused, energetic, intelligent, and adaptable.

Okay, so YOU tell me what that sounds like.

Well, to me it sounded like a good description of a squirrel. Squirrels are always high-energy and busy.

They are always very focused on the job at hand and rarely let anything throw them off task. They are pleasant little creatures who seem very involved with their own agendas and generally mean no harm to anyone. Squirrels just seem to be very busy all of the time and they definitely have a plan in mind.

See if any of these types of customers seem familiar to you...

The **Squirrel**

You know the Squirrels because they make up the vast majority of your customers.

These are the folks that you might not even notice because they are just going about their business.

If something is wrong they usually won't complain about it, unless it is a major problem. Normally, they do their thing without bothering anyone, including you. Squirrels are busy, have many things to get done and just want to keep moving along. They might ask a simple question or even nod at you as they hurry along with their appointed tasks.

Industrious, busy, determined, always-on-the-move, goal oriented, fast paced, focused, energetic, intelligent, adaptable.

The **Donkey**

The Donkey likes to let you hear about what is wrong without ever confronting you about it. Yep, he is the one that makes comments under his breath, but, just loud enough to make sure you hear it.

Stubborn and unwilling to do anything to improve the situation, the Donkey's braying sounds like this.

Stubborn, intolerant, close-minded, inflexible, negative, obstinate, one-sided, rigid, contrary, pessimistic, contradictory.

The **Junkyard Dogs**

The Junkyard Dogs are always a challenge to deal with. They are nasty to start with and they are sure to find something that is going to annoy them. In fact, it seems that they are actually looking for something to get upset about.

Once they have started barking they get themselves even more worked up and the whole process just seems to escalate. The Junkyard Dogs seem to like the sound of their own voices and can often adopt the attitude that they are owed complete satisfaction regardless of rules or reasonability.

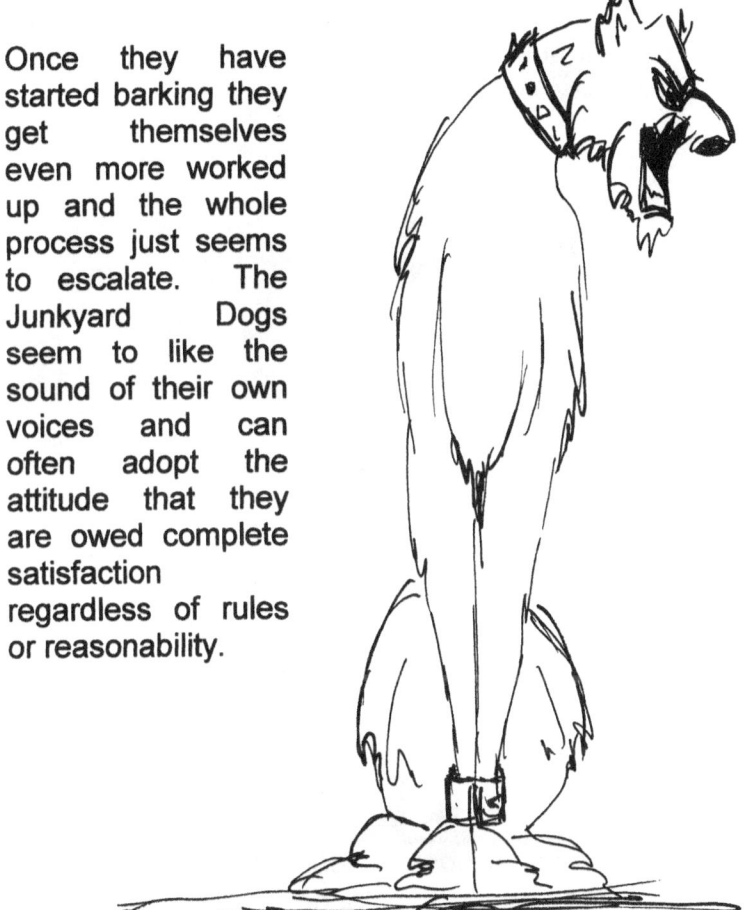

Mean, disagreeable, cruel, malicious, nasty, vicious, spiteful, excitable, vile, and ill tempered.

9

The **Peacocks**

The Peacocks strut around trying to believe in their own superiority. They seem to want to make others feel bad. Their noses (or beaks) are tipped slightly upward and they like to be very demanding, somehow figuring that being that way makes them more important. The normal offerings of your business will never be enough because they feel that they "deserve" special treatment.

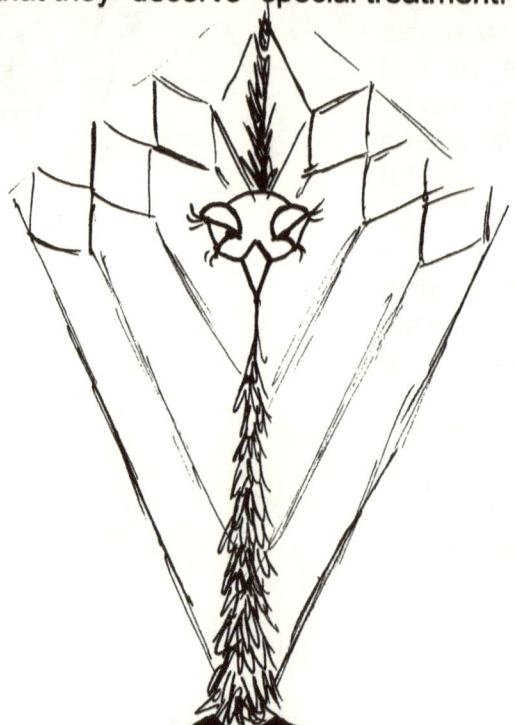

Aloof, indignant, arrogant, snobbish, egotistical, detached, conceited, haughty.

10

The **Bunnies**

Of course there are some really wonderful customers. People that you would willingly go out of your way for and enjoy doing it. The Bunnies are those special folks that it is a joy to help out. They are pleasant and appreciative of your efforts. It seems that there are never enough of these.

Friendly, agreeable, warm, likeable, pleasant, amiable, kind, gentle, good-natured.

Folks like the bunnies make us feel good about our job.

Is it any real mystery that we like to help, work with, talk to, spend time and interact with people who make us feel good about ourselves? Of course not.

Let's get real. When we are appreciated we feel better and we perform better. When customers are angry or unpleasant it makes our job that much more difficult. So, we are agreed then, that there are a wide variety of customers and it is our responsibility, our job, to take care of **all** of them.

Let me ask you a question at this point. We all know that in the real world Junkyard Dogs don't spontaneously turn into cute little Bunnies. But have you ever, *even once*, seen it happen in the Customer Service world? I have.

No, it doesn't happen often but it actually can *and* does happen. The transformation is almost as remarkable as it would be in the real world. In a little bit we will talk about the "magic" that can make that happen.

Linked Pairs

Let's take a look at probably the most important concept in this book...

It is what I call **"Linked Pairs"**....

Linked Pairs are the *Situations/Conditions* that cause a problem and the *Generally Appropriate Technique,* which can aid in solving it.

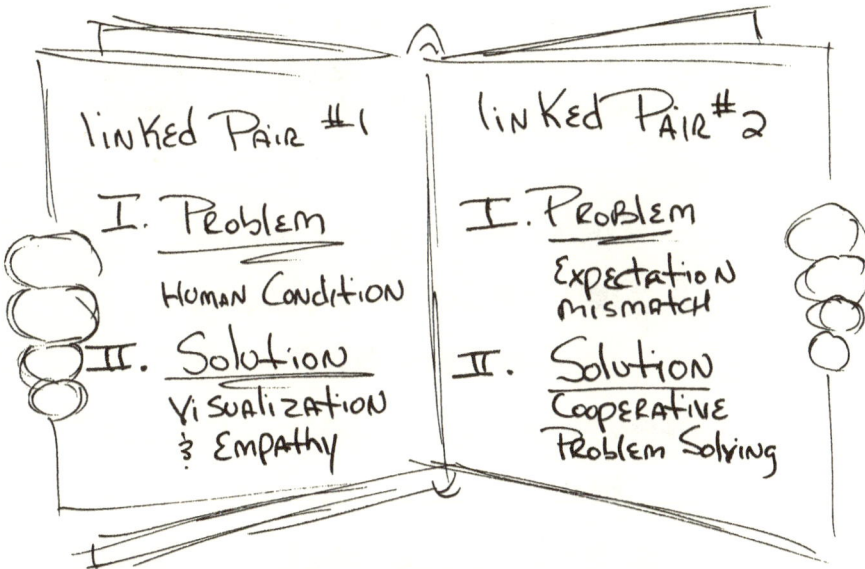

Something that is very important to note: although the Linked Pairs that I will present have a connection between the condition that is causing the problem and the generally appropriate technique for addressing the problem, it does not mean that you can't use either problem solving technique for either problem situation/condition!

The idea behind this concept is that when you identify what condition is causing the customer to have a problem (*Problem Causer*) you will then know the generally appropriate technique to apply to help solve the problem (*Problem Solver*).

The first **Linked Pair** we will examine is:

The Human Condition / Visualization and Empathy

The first Problem Causer is the **Human Condition.** OK, so what is the **Human Condition**?

Well, have you ever been in a "bad mood"?
Sure, all of us have. Take a moment and think back to a time when you were in a really bad mood. What made you that way?

A fight with your boss?

A sick child or relative?

Car trouble?

An argument with your spouse?

Money problems?

Didn't feel well?

Too much to do?

Feeling unappreciated?

The point is that something helped get you into that mood. Most people don't wake up and say...

"Today I want to be as miserable as possible".

There are lots of reasons that me, you, or anyone else can get into a bad mood. Yes, it is true that some of our customers seem to be in a bad mood all of the time. But what is the reason? Are they sick? Did someone they love pass away recently? Are they going through a break-up with a spouse? Is the reason they are so upset about that incorrect price because they are having severe financial difficulties?

I call these types of problems the **"Human Condition"**. They happen to everyone at one time or another. Some of us deal with them really well and others of us get very caught up in the problems. So the **Human Conditions** are the influences that all of us, as human beings, are susceptible to.

Therefore, whether your customer is a Bunny, a Squirrel or even a Junkyard Dog by nature they too are influenced by these **Human Conditions**!

OK, so if the **Human Condition** is causing the problem what is the solution?

In other words, what is the other half of this first "Linked Pair"? In this case the Problem Solver is **Visualization and Empathy.**

None of this stuff is hard to do, but it does take practice. And you know what? It works everytime. Why? Because it is all internal. It doesn't depend on your customer or their reaction. If you apply this technique correctly it can't fail because you are in control at all times.

Here is how the technique works...

Because we have all experienced the **Human Condition** it shouldn't be too difficult for us to **Visualize** a time in our own life when things were very difficult for us. Do you remember the feelings you had when you were turned down for that important job or promotion?

Can you recall a time when you got very disturbing medical news about a family member? Take a moment...really remember those emotions and how you felt. If you can begin to feel those feelings again then...

That is Visualization!

Now, after you have firmly recalled those emotions and feelings, is the time to begin to empathize. Wouldn't you have appreciated a little extra consideration at that moment? Do you think that perhaps your customer would also appreciate a little understanding too? When you remember how it felt and you understand that your customer might really just need someone to give him or her a break then...

That is Empathy!

Let's break down this technique a little. Once you have connected with the customer's **Human Condition** and have recalled your feelings in similar situations you can begin to address the problem.

This is done in just a few easy steps that I call the **3 V's**.

STEP ONE:
VALIDATION STATEMENT

The whole point of this step is to let your customer know that you recognize their point of view and to verbalize your concern and desire to help. This step is very important as it sets the tone for the rest of your interaction with the customer. Included are a few samples of Validation Statements, be sure to use only what feels comfortable and natural to you. There is nothing worse than for the customer to feel like you are simply giving them a "pat" answer or repeating a "line" you read somewhere (even here!).

As with everything in this book, you should take the ideas and incorporate them into your own customer service skill set.

" I think I can understand why you are upset...."
" It certainly makes sense that you would be angry..."
" I can see your point..."
" Yes, I agree with you...."
" I understand and I am here to help..."

Use your own words or some combination of these suggestions and your own ideas to **Validate** the feelings of your customer. Once they feel that you understand them (have empathy for them) they will be much easier to work with.

If you are **Visualizing** and **Empathizing** correctly, it will not be at all difficult to express your honest interest in solving the customer's problem.

Step Two: Verification

In step two, the 2nd V, the point is to correctly identify the problem you are going to help them with. One of the best methods to verify the customer's problem is to repeat it back to them. Not only does this illustrate that you are listening to them but it also shows your commitment to "getting it right".

While you are verifying the problem you might also get a hint from the customer as to what an appropriate solution might be. If you listen carefully customers almost always tell you what they were looking for before they became angry.

Step Three Vanquish

This is the meat of solving the problem. This step includes all of the problem solving techniques that you have already heard of. "Experience", "Thinking Outside of the Box", "Innovating" and all of the buzz words that, distilled down, simply mean finding a way (new, or tried and true) to solve the customer's problem.

An important, and sometimes overlooked, aspect of solving the problem is to check with the customer *after* you have offered your solution. If, and only if, the customer feels satisfied and is happy with the result will you have really vanquished the problem.

We can't know everything that our customers are dealing with, but we can empathize with them because we know that everyone has the same Human Conditions to deal with at one time or another.

Remember this technique works on all customer types, but let's take the Donkey customer as an example. Honestly, these folks used to drive me nuts. I just wanted to walk up to them and say...

"Look, obviously you have a problem. Why don't you just tell me what it is and maybe then I can do something about it. But grumbling under your breath isn't going to accomplish anything."

These donkey-people used to annoy me as much as the Junkyard Dogs. At least with the Junkyard Dogs you had the situation out in the open and stood a chance of turning things around.

Now lets apply Technique 1...**Visualization and Empathy**.

Here is what you hear the Donkey say....

I hate this place! They always run out of everything I can't believe how stupid these people are!

Wow, I don't know about you but that could really get me ticked off.

But then, I **Visualize** this person going through something difficult. The one that works for me the best is picturing that customer having just come from a funeral or wake. In my mind I try to see this person, maybe only minutes ago, feeling really sad about losing someone that they cared deeply about.

Another variation is to imagine that they, or someone they love, have just found out that they have a life-threatening medical condition. Picturing a very painful relationship breakup also works. I try to remember what my feelings were in a situation similar to that one.

20

Remember the **"Human Condition"**? As we said they are things that we all share, that we all go through at one time or another, so we all have those experiences to remember.

You have to put some effort into it, but try **Visualizing** a very painful moment from your own personal experiences and then **Empathize** with the customer by remembering how you felt. Think of them as having those same feelings right now.

Try this the next time you are in a tough customer situation...

Suddenly, almost magically, you start recognizing the truth; that there is something else that is bothering this person and that your store, department or group is just a convenient outlet for their bad feelings.

Does this make your customer a "bad person"? Of course not. Did it make you a bad person when you were going through a tough time? Remember back. Maybe you weren't as pleasant to others as you could have been either. What it means is that they, too, are human, dealing with the same **Human Conditions**, facing the same problems that you and I do.

So when you hear the donkey saying...

"I hate this place. They always run out of everything. I can't believe how stupid these people are."

Apply your newly learned **Visualization and Empathy** skill. Listen again, this time maybe even a little more closely. What you might really hear is...

> *"I am not very happy. There are things in my life right now that are very disturbing to me. Why can't things just be better for me? I wish someone would just give me a little break."*

When you hear it that way it is interesting how your whole perspective changes. The fact is that when you hear the "translation" it is probably closer to the truth than even your customer might realize!

Here is a simple real-life example of utilizing this technique. When I was employed as a District Manager for a movie theater chain I had the following occur.

It was a typically hectic Saturday night and most of the shows were quite busy. A family of three had purchased their tickets and had entered one of the theaters. I had noticed them as they came in. There was a father and mother both 50-60 years old and their son, in a wheel chair, who was probably in his mid-twenties but either a disease or an accident had left him unable to walk or talk. He did not appear to be in any pain but the face of his father was creased with many years of worry.

In just a few seconds the father came out of theater, which was dark by now as the show had already begun. This customer began by telling me how insensitive "we" were as a company since there were no places for disabled people to sit. I was a little confused because, in fact, we did have a section in the back of each of the theaters which was designed so that a person confined to a wheel chair could easily fit into it.

I thought he had just missed seeing it and I told him about the area. He said that he had seen it but he felt it was rude and insensitive to make them "sit in the back because they were disabled." I was amazed and a little insulted by the assumptions he was making.

An Important Hint....
It often happens that when the customer seems *very* unreasonable it is an indication that they are operating from within the **Human Condition** circumstance.

I was a little angry with this gentleman for suggesting that we were being discriminatory. It was equally unpleasant realizing that he didn't appreciate the efforts we had already made but then I began to apply the **Visualization** and **Empathy Technique.**

I tried to **Visualize/Empathize**, imagine the pain, both emotional and physical, the young man must have endured. I also tried to imagine the strain and sadness shouldered by the parents of this young man. I felt my defensiveness fading away. I thought to myself...

"I am sure that there are places that these customers have gone to in the past where the businesses have been less than sensitive."

I forced myself to see past the negative (and untrue) comments of this customer and listened instead to what his problem really was. In other words I was recognizing his **Human Condition**. He was hurt about his son, and who wouldn't have been?

23

I tried to explain about the fire codes and the idea we had employed in designing the theater, namely, that it would make both entering and leaving the theater easier for our disabled customers.

Honestly... I am not sure whether this really changed the father's mind at all or not. But two very important things happened. First, I was able to understand what was really causing him to act in the manner that he was. Secondly, I was able to deal with him in a polite, professional and, most importantly, an understanding way.

A basic concept of some eastern religions is the idea of attempting to lose one's ego. To stop thinking about the world in terms of how it relates to you and to start thinking of how life is affecting others. A very nice idea and something we should all learn to do much better.

Now the last thing I want is for everyone reading this book to start getting depressed because they are constantly thinking of horrible negative times in their lives or they are imagining customers going through painful life experiences.

The idea behind this technique is just to make us a little more tolerant and understanding of others. Personally, I don't think that compassion is overrated.

Remember **Linked Pair #1**. If you think that a customer's problem is because of a **Human Condition** then try the **Visualization and Empathy Technique.**

The second **Linked Pair** we will examine is:

Expectation Mismatch/Cooperative Problem Solving

If the **Human Condition** is one set of circumstances that can make our customers upset and our job more difficult, what could another set be?

Before we start, have you ever noticed how customers can sometimes be completely wrong?

Uh-Oh! I guess I just gave away my personal feelings about "The Customer is Always Right" philosophy.

My apologies to whomever first coined that phrase, but did they ever really work with customers? The fact is that customers *are* wrong sometimes and to say that they are not is either a serious breach of judgement or a lack of real-world experience.

Bestowing the benefit of the doubt to these authors, what I think they really meant to say was that the customer always deserves to be treated with respect, or maybe even that the customer always deserves our honest and best attempt to make them happy.

I couldn't agree more with those ideas. The simple truth, however, is that the customer is wrong sometimes.

Sometimes it is their fault, sometimes it is ours and sometimes it is just a set of circumstances and no one's fault at all, and that is where **Expectation Mismatch** comes in.

25

When the customer expects one thing and gets something else, that is **Expectation Mismatch.** **Expectation Mismatch** happens often and the reasons for it are many, like:

✓ Misprinted, conflicting or ambiguous advertisements.
✓ Misinformation provided by someone who is unaware of the actual facts.
✓ Simple misunderstanding.

Some examples might be:

✓ Your customer shows up for a meeting a day early.
✓ The special price your customer came in for ended yesterday.
✓ The advertisement that your customer read was for a different company.
✓ You are "sold out" of the item the customer wanted.
✓ The specifications of the product are not what your customer thought they were.
✓ Your customer thought that they would have received their shipment a week ago.

Borrowing from the **Visualization** and **Empathy** technique for a moment…

Were **YOU** ever wrong?

Yep, here we go again. I am not going to present this process to you all over again. I am sure you understand my point. Just like with the **Human Condition** we all have run into this before ourselves.

Here it is, a Hugely Important Concept...

Customers that appear unreasonable are really just like you and me when we are having a bad day!

27

Lets take a look at the second half of **Linked Pair #2**....
a technique that I call, **Cooperative Problem Solving**.

This is one of my personal favorites. There are actually
five parts or phases to this technique but they can all
occur within seconds. Let's look at them as a group and
then examine each one in just a little more detail.

> Introduction to the challenge
> Investigation of the challenge
> Initiation of the team
> Innovate solutions
> Interpretation of results

These five **I's** are the foundation for the **Cooperative
Problem Solving** technique. Again, nothing very
difficult at all to this approach...in fact, you already do
some of these every time you interact with a customer!

Introduction Phase

This is actually the first moment of contact with the
customer and it is very important. At this point sincerity,
and a real desire to help, them needs to be
demonstrated. Also of importance is communicating a
sense of calm and an air of self–assuredness. In those
first few seconds the customer needs to feel that you are
taking their situation seriously *and* that you will do
something to solve the problem. Here is a little hint.
Take a small pad of paper with you and begin to write
down everything that they are telling you. This clearly
illustrates that you are very concerned, concerned
enough to "take note" of what they are saying.

Investigation Phase

During this phase you are going to investigate the problem, in depth. Try to gently control the discussion by asking questions that are going to help you identify the core issue(s). You can't help the customer if you don't understand what they want and what the problem is. Listening skills are critical here! Take your time. Don't jump to conclusions.

Initiation Phase

This is the most important phase of this whole process. The main concept here is that you make the customer feel that <u>both of you are on the same team</u> and that your mutual goal is to solve the problem. This can't be overstated. You must make them sense that you are on their side and that your desire is to solve the problem with them. Remember it is **you** and the **customer** vs. the problem.

Innovation Phase

Solutions are the key here. Think "outside of the box" and be creative. Attempt to understand what the customer really needs, there may be other ways to accomplish the same thing. You must identify possible solutions and then present them to the customer.

Interpretation Phase

Once solutions are offered, be certain to evaluate the customer's reaction. During this phase you are going to interpret the customer's level of satisfaction and their demeanor.

It can't hurt to ask the question... "Does this seem fair to you?" Or even... "Is this Okay with you?".

An unsatisfied customer who has had a bad experience is bad enough, but one that feels that you were unwilling to help them is even worse.

Let's use an example to walk through this...

This is an actual example of a relatively little situation that seemed like a big deal, at least to one customer.

I was working as the Night Manager for a large supermarket chain. This was the type of store that had everything in it, from a restaurant to a pharmacy, a photo department to a video store, as well as thousands and thousands of fresh and standard grocery items. As the Night Manager, I was in charge of the facility during the evening hours. I had a call from our Service Desk telling me that they had a very irate customer. I, of course, went to see if I could help. Here is what happened...

Introduction Phase

I said… "Good Evening… I am here to help."

Notice, I didn't ask what the problem was yet, I told the customer that I was there to help him. I took out my notepad and got ready to write. I was trying to keep the situation as light as possible and yet, demonstrate that my job and my commitment was to solve his problem.

The customer, an older gentleman, was very upset at this point. He had come into the store to purchase garbage bags. (In this city you have to use specific bags or the city crews will not pick them up. Our store bought them from the city and then re-sold them to our customers as a convenience.)

Investigation Phase

I asked. "Can you tell me what is wrong?"

Now, I am asking the customer what the problem is. The customer immediately went into a tirade about the fact that we had the bags for sale but that we didn't have the extra long twist ties that normally come with them. This was an easy one. It didn't take too much probing to get to the core issue for this particular problem.

Continuing with the investigation phase I asked our employees why this had happened. They explained that the last batch of bags that the city supplied to us did not come with the twist ties. OK, so now another problem had been identified and that too would have to be addressed.

31

Unfortunately, that information didn't calm down the customer at all. Truthfully, I was a little amazed that this was that big of a deal. After all you could simply tie the corners of the bags together but I recognized that this gentleman was upset regardless of whether I thought it was important or not.

At this point, it was clear that there was a difference between what we could provide and what the customer expected, **Expectation Mismatch**. On one hand, it was certainly not our fault that the city had failed to provide us with the ties, but on the other, it was our responsibility to do whatever we could to accommodate the customer.

Initiation Phase

I said. "Well that's not good. Our customers won't want to buy the bags without them and we can't give them the ties if they haven't been given to us."

As you might notice, I am now putting the customer and myself in the same boat. **It is critical that I make him see that we BOTH have the same problem.** In this case, no twist ties! A point of clarification here, we don't want to try to blame someone else. That just seems lame. That's why I did not say something like, *"That's the city for you, they never get anything right."* We want to communicate our agreement, with the customer, that there is a problem.

Remember when we talked about the Junkyard Dogs and how sometimes nothing seems to get them calmed down?

Well, this gentleman never even gave me a chance to go into the Innovation phase. He grabbed the bags he had just purchased and stormed off into the store muttering all the way.

Innovation Phase

Between you and I, at that moment I was having trouble seeing why this was such a major concern. But, obviously, to that customer it was very important and in providing excellent customer service what is important to your customer MUST be important to you. As I have already mentioned I could think of several ways to keep his garbage bag closed, from tying it off, to using masking tape, but that was not the core problem.

This customer wanted his twist ties. So, now, with the proper identification of the problem I proceeded to innovate or brainstorm a solution. Here is what I came up with.

Like all of the really big grocery store chains we had a pretty extensive Produce Department. In that dept we had twist ties. Not the giant long ones that this customer was expecting, but a shorter version of the same thing. My solution was embarrassingly simple. I went back to the Produce Department took a handful of these ties and then began twist tying them together end-to-end to make several longer versions. This only took a minute or so and I returned to find the customer in our checkout lines. I took the "homemade" giant twist ties over to him.

33

Interpretation Phase

I said to the customer… "I know these aren't exactly what you were looking for but I think they might do the trick." I also said… "I will get in touch with the folks we buy the bags from and make sure that we get an extra supply in as soon as possible."

Remember back a few pages when we talked about seeing the magic of a Junkyard Dog turning into a Bunny? Well, that is exactly what happened. The customer looked at me and said…*"Uh, umm, well, thanks for going to all that trouble".*

Honestly, I think that he might have felt a little silly about making such a big deal out of twist ties. I continued the Interpretation Phase by asking…*"Do you think these will work for you? We should have more of the regular twist ties in tomorrow."*

He said that they would work fine and then thanked me again. By letting this customer "overhear" the fact that the twist ties came from the supplier (the city) he was now aware of the process involved on our end, this aids in eliminating misunderstanding and the **Mismatch of Expectations**.

Certainly, we don't want to "lecture" the customer but we do need to make them aware of our procedures. If we are all on the same page it will make our interactions that much easier. If you want a fun way to think about it, realize this… You are actually teaching the customer technique number 1 to **Visualize and Empathize** with you!

Now that was a very simple version of applying the **Cooperative Problem Solving** technique, but I think you get the idea.

Here is the whole idea of **Cooperative Problem Solving**, in a nutshell,

It is essentially siding with the customer so that they feel a sense of...

"You <u>and</u> the Customer vs. the Problem"

"The Customer vs. you (the Organization)"

Instead Of

It is also creative problem solving, thinking "outside of the box" and innovative solutions.

Examples and Review

Okay, Time for a quick review!

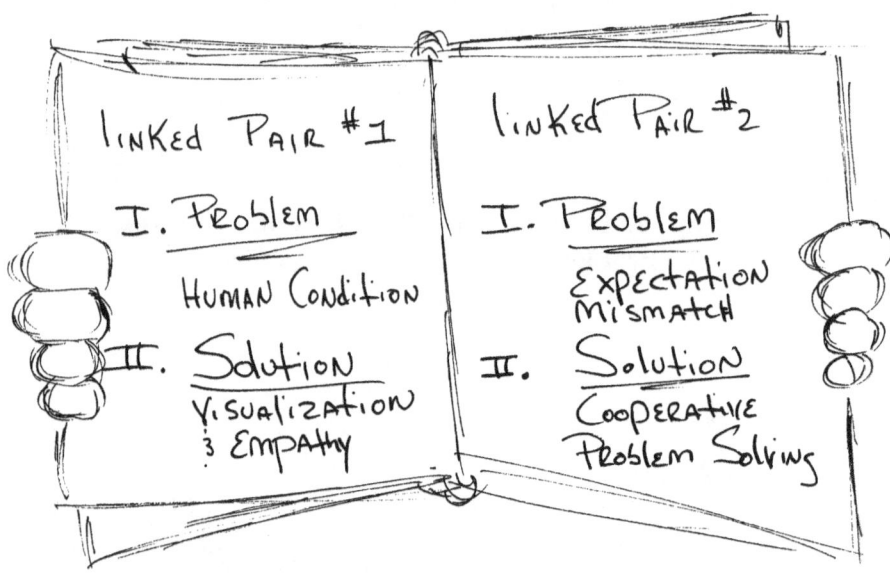

As we talked about earlier it is important to note that applying a technique different from what is indicated above is Okay!

Applying a technique different from what is indicated above is Okay!

Sometimes we need to repeat things to ourselves to get the message across.

No one can tell as much about the situation as you, especially when you are in the middle of it. There is another point that needs to be made too.

Sometimes people do not necessarily fall neatly into only one of the circumstances listed above. In the real world there definitely could be a mixture of circumstances that produce a "challenge" situation.

Our job is to be sensitive to all of the circumstances that a customer might have occurring and to be prepared to try any techniques to satisfy the customer.

OK, so now we have identified the two main circumstances or reasons problems exist the **Human Condition** and **Expectation Mismatch** and we have also looked at two techniques **Visualization/Empathy** and **Cooperative Problem Solving** to help address these problems.

Let's do a quick exercise to see if you can spot the problem.

Presented next are one-line scenario's… you decide which circumstance the customer is operating from **Human Condition** or **Expectation Mismatch**.

Remember, identify the "*problem causer*" and choose the appropriate "*problem solver*".

Which circumstance or condition do you think *most likely* exists for each of the scenarios below?

Human Condition or **Expectation Mismatch**.

✓ A customer is unusually upset about having to wait in line. *"Forever in Line…"*

✓ A customer yells at you because their shipment has not yet arrived. *"Where the heck…?"*

✓ A customer is angry that you are "out-of-stock" on a sale item. *"Oops, we got no bananas…"*

✓ A customer complains that one of your departments' closes way too early. *"You are NOT open 24/7…?"*

✓ Her child is screaming. The customer is upset that you need to see her check-cashing card. *"Mommy, mommy, mommy…"*

As you can see, there are ways that each of these could fall into both categories but generally here are the most likely answers:

✓ *"Forever in Line"…*Human Condition

✓ *"Where the heck"…*Expectation Mismatch

✓ *"Oops, we got no bananas"…*Expectation Mismatch

✓ *"You are NOT open 24/7"…*Expectation Mismatch

✓ *"Mommy, mommy, mommy"…*Human Condition

Very good. Since we have been able to identify the circumstance, the "problem causer", lets take a look at the appropriate response, the "problem solver".

✓ *"Forever in Line"*...**Visualization/Empathy**

✓ *"Where the heck"*...**Cooperative Problem Solving**

✓ *"Oops, we got no bananas"*... **Cooperative Problem Solving**

✓ *"You are NOT open 24/7"*... **Cooperative Problem Solving**

✓ *"Mommy,mommy,mommy"*...**Visualization/Empathy**

In the name of brevity let's give a short answer using the techniques to see how they work.

"Forever in Line..."
Say to the customer... "I know how you feel. Waiting in line drives me crazy sometimes. When we have long lines it just stresses out the employees and the customers and everyone ends up unhappy. I might be able to help though. When you are finished shopping, let me know. I can hold on to your packages while you drive your car up. Then I can help you load up the car and that way you can get out of here a little faster.

"Where the heck..."
Say to the customer... "Let me see if I can help. When was the shipment supposed to be there and if you have an order number I can track it down for you. I will call you back in 15 minutes to tell you what I have found out. Maybe we can even get an express package out to you so you could have the parts you need as soon as possible."

"Oops, we got no bananas..."

Say to the customer... "I am sorry we are out that item. We certainly are in the business to sell the product and if we don't have them in then, we are in trouble. I do have a solution for you though... How about if we give you a "raincheck" for this item and I think I have a great substitute right over here, which I could offer you at the same price. Do you think that would work out for you?"

"You are NOT open 24/7..."

Say to the customer... "Yes, unfortunately we do close that department at 8:00pm. We tried staying open later but, we just didn't have enough business. It certainly would be a lot more convenient to have it open later. I will pass your comments on to the store manager. For now though, if you would like, I could get you a copy of the times that our individual departments close. Would that be helpful?"

"Mommy, mommy, mommy..."

Say to the customer... "I am sorry to have to bug you for this. Can I hold something for you? Then look at the child and create a diversion by saying... "How old are you? or "And what is your name?" We have all seen this one done before.

Now these are really, really short answers and the problems would probably be more complicated than our examples here. In fact, I am sure you already saw how, depending upon how you read it, you could have easily labeled the first scenario, "Forever in Line"...as **Expectation Mismatch**.

40

Now that we have established the concept of **Linked Pairs** you will be able to evaluate any given situation and then begin to respond with either the **Visualization/Empathy** or the **Cooperative Problem Solving** technique.

Remember no matter which technique you use...solving the customers' problem to their satisfaction is the most important part. You may need to use a combination of both techniques in some instances.

At this point I am sure some people are saying...

"Okay, I can give this a try. It can't hurt. But some customers are REALLY difficult to please and what do I do if I can't figure out whether they are upset about a **Human Condition** *or an* **Expectation Mismatch***?"*

It is fair to say that sometimes you might not be able to figure out which circumstance a customer is coming from, that is to say, that you don't know whether the problem is a **Human Condition** or an **Expectation Mismatch.** Hopefully that will not happen often and the more you practice figuring it out, the better you get at it. Trust me! So what do you do in those cases? Well...

Just like the **Linked Pairs** between a "problem causer" or condition and a "problem solver" or technique, there are some basic **Linked Pairs** between the **Customer Type** and the generally appropriate technique to use in dealing with them.

A Word of Warning!

41

This is a little trickier. It asks us to correctly identify the **Customer Type.** As we all know sometimes the sweetest looking little elderly lady, who you would assume to be a cute little Bunny, really turns out to be a full-fledged, card carrying Junkyard Dog.

Do you remember the five Customer Types?

CUSTOMER TYPES AND TECHNIQUE LINKS

The Squirrels, the Donkeys, the Junkyard Dogs,
the Peacocks, the Bunnies.

Lets look at each one and try to figure out which approach would probably work better.

<u>IMPORTANT NOTE</u>: This exercise assumes that you **can't** figure out whether they are operating from a **Human Condition** or an **Expectation Mismatch**.

Let's tackle the Junkyard Dogs first.

Since this is not rocket science, you tell me which technique you think would work best on a customer with the temperament of a Junkyard Dog.

Try this …picture that Junkyard Dog (on the other side of a fence for safety). There you are trying to **Visualize / Empathize** with it. You are saying you understand why he is so upset, you are talking in calming tones, and you are trying to understand what it feels like to be that nasty.
And what does the Junkyard Dog do?
Yep, he barks all the more!

Another old saying ... *"You can't make a silk purse out of a sow's ear"*

The Junkyard Dog customer type is rarely going to be satisfied by **Empathy**. The only thing that is going to calm him down is for the situation to change, namely in this case, for you to leave. After you are gone, he will still be barking for a few minutes but then eventually he will calm down all on his own. So throw him a bone (or the solution) and get out of there!

The obvious suggestion here is that **Visualization/ Empathy** *generally* won't work on a Junkyard Dog. That doesn't mean it never works but usually you are better off approaching a Junkyard Dog with the **Cooperative Problem Solving** technique.

Let's look at another example...

What if a Bunny customer type had a problem?

Well, by their nature Bunnies are going to be appreciative of just about anything you do so this takes a little of the pressure off. However there actually is a better technique to use with them.

How would a Bunny customer type react to the following...?

You, in an effort to help them, come directly up to them and immediately get down to the business of solving the problem. You begin to apply the **Cooperative Problem Solving** technique asking questions, probing for the problem, offering alternatives. Now, in many cases, as I said, they will be appreciative of your efforts. But, imagine this conversation between the Bunny and a friend of his.

"Yes, I was in the store and I had this problem. The manager came up to me, she was very nice, but she just seemed to be in a big hurry. Before I could even tell her how I was feeling she had already offered a solution and was off to take care of something else. She was nice but, I felt like I was just another one of many problems she was solving that day."

Again, it is not always the case that the Bunny **Customer Type** will prefer the **Visualization/Empathy** technique but in most cases they will.

Of course it goes without saying that they still want the problem resolved but often how it is handled is just as important as the actual solution.

Okay, so let's finish up the list...

A couple of quick notes to explain the last 3...

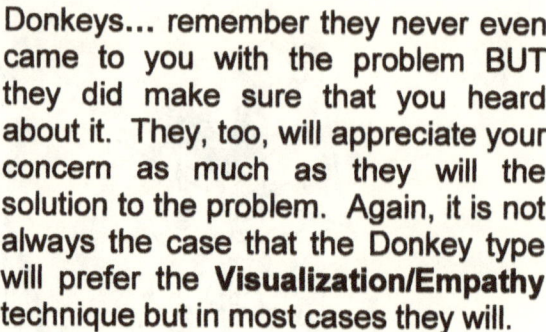

Donkeys... remember they never even came to you with the problem BUT they did make sure that you heard about it. They, too, will appreciate your concern as much as they will the solution to the problem. Again, it is not always the case that the Donkey type will prefer the **Visualization/Empathy** technique but in most cases they will.

Peacocks...this customer type needs to be treated with some special attention. Simply solving a problem for them will not satisfy their need to be treated in an "above average" sort of way. Again the preferred technique is **Visualization/Empathy**.

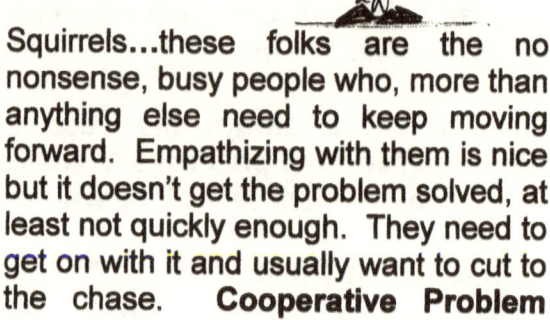

Squirrels...these folks are the no nonsense, busy people who, more than anything else need to keep moving forward. Empathizing with them is nice but it doesn't get the problem solved, at least not quickly enough. They need to get on with it and usually want to cut to the chase. **Cooperative Problem Solving** is the technique of choice when dealing with the Squirrels.

In Review....

Customer Type   Technique

Junkyard Dogs ———►   Cooperative Problem Solving

Squirrels   ———►   Cooperative Problem Solving

Bunnies   ———►   Visualization/Empathy

Donkeys   ———►   Visualization/Empathy

Peacocks   ———►   Visualization/Empathy

It is always better to determine which set of circumstances a customer is coming from, whether it is the **Human Condition** or **Expectation Mismatch** simply because people can be very situation specific. Today, I might be operating from a **Human Condition** and tomorrow it might very well be **Expectation Mismatch** that is causing my problem.

So *always* attempt to figure out which circumstance they are coming from FIRST.

THEN, if that doesn't work, match the broader categories of **Customer Type** with the proper technique.

Wow, we have talked about a lot of stuff! Let's take a breather.

Do you know what prompted me to write this book?

Not dreams of being rich and famous.
Although I certainly wouldn't mind that!

Not trying to set myself up as an expert.
Everyone has great ideas on providing excellent customer service, obviously not just me.

Not even imagining people using these ideas.
Who knows for sure how this will be received?

No, the real reason was simply this...

I thought it was time for an honest discussion about customer service...and how difficult it can be to do the job.

Quite frankly, I was tired of hearing people complaining about the "bad service" they received. I was constantly amazed how many people complained about it but how few did anything about it. I was tired of hearing the old cliché "the customer is always right" when I knew for a fact (and so do you) that this is simply not true.

How can any business truly expect their employees to do their best when they start off by force feeding them a silly concept that is obviously wrong?

Actually, I am working on an idea for another book, one that you might be able to participate in...

It is called (tentatively) "Our Turn" and it is a listing of the nightmarish examples of totally unreasonable customers. We always hear the stories of customers who have gotten "bad service" but how about telling the story of the people giving the customer service and the things that *they* have had to endure?

So if you would like to send me your customer service story for consideration, just email me at:

AimforExcellence@aol.com

Well, enough advertising for now.

We only have a few more ideas to go over so let's get to it.

Opportunities for Excellence

Providing excellent customer service is in some ways much like baseball.

Every time you get up to bat *(have an encounter with a customer)* you have the opportunity for a home run *(excellent customer service)*. Are you going to "hit-one-out-of-the-park" every time? No. But, as long as you don't strike out you are moving closer to winning the game. Even the lesser success of a base hit is still a success!

In fact, these smaller accomplishments give you the experience you need to fine-tune your swing *(customer service technique)* so that eventually you will have the bases loaded *(lots of smaller successes)* and you will be ready when the opportunity presents itself for a grand slam *(Excellence in Customer Service)*.

These encounters are what I call **Opportunities for Excellence** because you never know when the moment will present itself for that Grand Slam *(a customer who is overwhelmed by your customer service skills)*. What a super feeling it is when you connect and that ball goes sailing out of the park *(when the customer looks at you and says.. "I am amazed at how awesome you are at customer service!")*.

Opportunities for Excellence occur daily. Let me tell you two brief stories about **Opportunities for Excellence.**

Here is a very simple little story. *I was shopping with my wife, Doreen and my two children, Nicholas and Kelly at a major retail-shopping store. Honestly, I was not very impressed with the customer service skills that were being demonstrated (as a matter of fact that evening was the 1st time that I sat down and started to write this book). My children were 9 and 4 years old at the time this occurred.*

We had been shopping for some "back-to-school" items and as we were getting ready to check out my littlest one, Kelly, asked if she could have a drink. I looked over and saw a small luncheonette area which sold hot dogs, slush drinks, nachos and other items.

I took my son, Nicholas, with me and we went over to the counter, where we waited for a few minutes before the lady working in that area noticed us. While I was waiting I was looking around at all of the advertisements and specials that they offered. My kids had wanted one of those slush-type drinks and I noticed that they had coupons sitting on the counter, which offered a small popcorn "free" with the purchase of any slush drink.

When the woman finally came over to us I ordered 2 of the slush drinks and purposely waited to see if she would mention the special. She, of course, did not. So, being a savvy shopper myself, I inquired about it. She said, "Oh, yes". Now, certainly it is possible that she simply forgot (I would be pretty hypocritical if I didn't Empathize with her now wouldn't I?). But, my point here, is the number of **Opportunities for Excellence** *that she missed, as you will soon see.*

When she finally did get the drinks she forgot to get the popcorn for us. So, I had to mention it again. So, here I was having a mildly negative experience, when it all should have gone so much better.

Here is what could have happened...
She certainly should have been aware that someone was entering her department and even if she wasn't she could have said something to acknowledge my waiting for her. Something like...

"Oh, I am sorry I was just cleaning up out back. I hope I didn't keep you waiting too long."

With a simple statement like that I would have immediately known that she was concerned about the level of service she was offering her customers. As it was she neither acknowledged it nor apologized for causing me to wait. The end of the world? No, but to continue with the baseball analogy...strike number one.

The employee should have been aware of the "specials" that were going on at the time, especially considering that the coupons were on the counter not more than 8 inches from the register. If she were aware she could have happily said....

"Just so that you know, we have a special right now. With every drink that you purchase you get a free bag of popcorn! Would you like that?

Once again let's give her the benefit of the doubt and say that something very important was weighing on her mind and that she had forgotten about the special. Has she lost a customer for life? No, but strike number two. What should she have done when I mentioned it to her? How about...

"I am so glad you saw that. My head must be somewhere else today. Yes, it is a really good deal. I would be happy to get that for you."

After she got the drinks some of the product had spilled down the side and on the bottom of the cup. Instead of wiping it up and saying something like...

"Here let me get this cleaned up..."

...she just handed it to me and I had to get a napkin and wipe it up myself!

Remember now that she had forgotten *again* after she got the drinks to get the popcorn and I had to remind her. Did the whole store stop and notice this? Nope, but strike number three.

Once again a simple statement of recognition of her mistake would have made all of the difference. It is simple human nature to forgive someone if they admit the mistake and are genuinely apologetic. That's because of the **Human Condition**, we have all, at one time or another, been the person making the mistake before.

So after another prompting she gave us the bags of popcorn (with Giant Size) written on the side. I can only assume that they had run out of the small bags, which were part of the promotion. At least she didn't tell me that I couldn't have the special because they had run out of the small bags. But once again she missed an **Opportunity for Excellence**.

She could have said...

"We are all out of the small bags that we are supposed to use so I am going to give you the giant size instead!"

My thought, even with everything else that she had done wrong, would have been something like...

"Well that is nice of her to do that."

And I am certain I would have mentioned that to my son and thanked her as well. All of these were missed **Opportunities for Excellence** which together made for a very unsatisfying shopping experience. Now in the grand scheme of things was any part of that a "big deal"? No, not really, except when you consider the missed opportunities. Once again it was not the situation but the way in which it was handled that caused the negative feelings.

The next story is another personal experience. In fact it happened just shortly after I began to write this book. Being aware and keeping customer service in the forefront of our minds will always help us to perform at a higher level. This also occurred in a major grocery store chain that I was working for.

As I was walking across the front register area of our store I saw an older couple walking toward me. The husband seemed fine but his wife was sweating profusely and seemed very upset. I heard her say as they came closer to me..."Please just ask someone for help".

As I looked at her it was clear she was VERY upset about something. Because she was so upset I was worried that she might end up needing medical attention. Partly out of breath, she said…"Do you work here?"

I told her "Yes" and I asked what I could help with. When she told me the story I very slowly, calmly and "matter-of-factly" said…"Listen now, everything is going to be OK. You are here now and, no matter what, we will get the situation resolved. I promise."

There was a look of relief but still a twinge of doubt in her face. I looked at her again and said…"I promise."

Let me have this sweet lady tell you the story in her own words. This is compiled from a call to the company I was working for.

She wanted to be sure that her compliments were passed on to the right people. She said, "My husband and I were travelling from New York City. We stayed at the Inn in Corning and went to the Corning Glass Center. We parked at the top level of a parking garage while in the Glass Center.

When we got back to our car, the remote to open the car doors would not work. Someone suggested we walk down to your grocery super store to get a new battery for the remote. It was a pretty far walk. My husband is 83 and I am 75. When we got there, we were helped by a man named Tim Bonomo.

Tim opened the remote case for my husband. We could not get it open. Tim found the right battery and put it in for my husband. We told Tim where we parked. He offered to give us a ride because it was a long walk. Can you imagine this generous man? He didn't even know us, but that isn't the half of it.

When he got us to our car we found that my husband had left the lights on and the car battery was dead. It was not the remote at all. Tim had waited to be sure everything was okay. At this point Tim got his cables and jumped our car for us. He then asked where we were staying and insisted that he follow us back to the Inn to be sure that we got there safely. Again I ask you can you imagine the kindness of a perfect stranger? I used to work for Phillip Morris. I have traveled all over the world and never, ever have I experienced this type of unselfish kindness. You would have thought this man was helping his very own mother and father. I am forever grateful and I wanted to be sure that you knew about this. Thank you for listening to me and thank you, Tim!

Please don't misunderstand my telling you this story. It is not my intention to pat myself on the back. Many people have great customer service stories. The idea of *both* of these stories is to show that the **Opportunity for Excellence** presents itself almost daily and that customers really do appreciate your efforts!

Thanks for sticking with me so far! We have two more concepts that I would like to talk about briefly. These are the foundation of ongoing, excellent customer service. Without them all of the techniques and ideas that you have learned about are just theory and pretty much wasted.

Everyday Extraordinary Service

"God is in the details..."

Everyday Extraordinary Service is the one of the last areas that I want to discuss and it is very important. It deals with the basic idea that most businesses, of a particular type, offer very similar products and/or services. Take a look at fast food chains for example. Most offer several types of burgers, chicken of some sort, a fish sandwich, french-fries, milk shakes, soft drinks, desert pies. The menu is virtually identical with only a very few variations here and there.

The point here is that when very large competitors offer similar products at virtually identical prices the only way to "stand out" is with **Everyday Extraordinary Service**. Obviously, from my perspective, Customer Service is the most important way to illustrate the differences between you and your competitors and **Everyday Extraordinary Service** is the method for making that happen. This is similar to **Opportunities for Excellence** but instead of having a situation happen and then finding the best way to maximize your Customer Service response, **Everyday Extraordinary Service** is apparent in each and every transaction or interaction with your customer.

Here is an example... do you remember the very first time you stayed at a hotel where they leave those great little chocolates on your pillow? It was years ago but I remember it vividly. The first time that I saw that little gift I was quite impressed. I thought it was extraordinary, wonderful and a very nice touch.

Now, was it incredibly expensive? No. Did it take an inordinate amount of time? No. But the effect was quite profound. In fact I would say that most "excellence in customer service" does *not* take a long time, does *not* cost a lot of money and really requires relatively little extra effort.

So we know that another method for providing excellence in customer service is **Everyday Extraordinary Service** and attention to the details, but how do we go about doing that? Well the answer, just like everything else that you have learned, is surprisingly simple.

Every job has basic components. For a cashier it would be accurately and efficiently being able to process a transaction and knowing the policies and specials. But now think about the best cashiers you have ever interacted with. They do all of that almost invisibly and then they add on **Everyday Extraordinary Service**, the details. Make no mistake about it...to accomplish this component of excellent customer service does require a little extra effort but the payoff is incredible. This is exactly the opposite of the Law of Diminishing Returns. With **Everyday Extraordinary Service** you can expect to get a 5 to 1 payoff minimum...odds any bookie would love.

To make it really simple, there are really only 2 parts to remember to **Everyday Extraordinary Service**

Observation of the Customer's Needs
Reaction to the Customer's Needs

I probably should state for the record that these "customer needs" are not the same as the usual expectations that a customer has. Let's go back to the cashier example. All customers reasonably expect that a cashier understands and can provide the basics such as:

✓ greeting the customer,
✓ being able to correctly ring out an order,
✓ packing or wrapping the items, and
✓ the closing or thanking the customer.

It is also reasonable to assume that the cashier can do this with at least a decent attitude. So what happens when someone is committed to **Aiming for Excellence**? Here is a scenario with two different levels of customer service, which do you think the customer would most likely talk about after she left your business?

An older woman comes in to purchase some groceries. Let's say that she doesn't buy a lot of items but easily fills 2 good size bags full.

Cashier *without* **Everyday Extraordinary Service.**

"Hi" Rings up order. Makes change. Packs groceries in 2 bags. "Thank you". Customer leaves.

Now nothing really negative happened here, but nothing **Extra ordinary** either. Customer is marginally satisfied. But what could have happened?

Cashier *with* **Everyday Extraordinary Service.**

"Good morning! How are you this morning?" Rings up order. *"Did you find everything you were looking for ma'am?"* Makes change. *"Is it still chilly outside?"* *"Would you like me to pack these a little lighter for you?"* *"If you would like, I can get someone to help you to your car with these; it's really no problem..."* *"Have a great day!"* *"Hope to see you again soon!"*

How do you feel about the two experiences? And which would you rather see your customers experience? In all honesty there are opportunities for more problems to arise in the second scenario; but aren't these the things that you want to know about so that you can fix them?

In scenario # 2 the cashier is going beyond standard customer service. She might even be creating a little more work for herself but the experience she gives to her customer is invaluable. What would you expect the little old lady to say about scenario # 1? Right. Nothing.

And scenario # 2? Well maybe she still won't say anything... but at the least isn't she thinking... *"My what a nice young lady."*

Or maybe even... *"You see that is why I shop there...they are all so nice."*

Isn't that the point of aiming for excellence in customer service?

What if she actually says one of those things to your cashier or tells someone else the story of her shopping experience?

If we break down the cashier's **Everyday Extraordinary Service** what do we see?

In the **Observation** part of this exercise the cashier is looking to see what needs the customer might have.

First, she is doing more than saying "hello" she is engaging the customer in a conversation. Secondly, she is anticipating any needs this customer might have, such as items that she wanted but could not find.

Next, she continues the person-to-person interaction with the customer and follows it up with an even greater level of anticipation of this particular customer's needs. She is an older woman, wouldn't it be easier for her if she had the bags packed a little lighter? Also wouldn't she appreciate having someone carry and load her groceries into her car for her?

Telling her to have a great day and saying that she hopes to see her again soon can only make the customer feel both recognized and appreciated.

Our cashier successfully **Observed** the needs of this customer and her **Reaction** is to offer solutions, namely lighter bags, a helping hand, etc.

Simply put:

Everyday Extraordinary Service
=
Extraordinary Results Everyday

Professionalism

Some people think it is funny that I would mention professionalism, especially when I am talking about customer service. Folks mistakenly think that professionalism is the exclusive territory of doctors, lawyers and the like and they couldn't possibly be more wrong!

It really doesn't matter how old or how young you are, whether you are an executive, a member of middle management or one of the many front line employees, professionalism should always be your goal.

Professionalism is the degree of skill and the level of commitment that you approach your job with, whatever that job may be!

For a cook it is their culinary skills. For an administrative assistant it would be their office expertise. For an accountant it might be your bookkeeping proficiency. It is how important all of this is to you that determines how good of a job you do. If there is no commitment then you are doing nothing more than putting in your time to get paid.

It is no accident that the people who excel in their jobs have a high level of professionalism. So how do we achieve professionalism?

People say that copying someone is the highest form of flattery, so my suggestion is to seek out the person you consider to be the most professional at their job (hopefully it will be someone in a similar position to yours, but that is not absolutely necessary) and copy them.

Observe them first watch how they handle every single moment of their interaction with the customer. Take notes. Evaluate. Ask questions. On the following page are some trademark characteristics of people who illustrate true professionalism. I think you will find that the person you have identified, as the "most professional person you know" will have many, if not all, of the following characteristics.

 The professional is always aware of his/her customer and tries to give them what they want and need. The professional is always interested in the customer and is actually "standing by" ready to help. Being aware of your surroundings is very important. Professionals are not like vultures ready to pounce but more like an operating room nurse, ready to help and anticipating the doctor's (and the patient's) needs.

The  professional always interacts with their client or customer in a positive and supportive way. They don't necessarily have to rush up to the customer but they let the customer know that they are engaged in the interaction and look forward to interacting with them. This can be as simple as a smile and a nod or by saying, "Hi, how are you today?" You can't be helpful or professional without interacting with the customer on some level.

P
o
i
s
e
d
Any really professional person always keeps things on an "even keel". They are calm and steady and they know they can handle anything that comes their way. They are self-assured. There is no reason to get all emotionally supercharged if you know that you can handle the situation. Think of it this way, getting all emotional with an emotional person just makes the situation...well....even more emotional!

I have never met one truly **Committed** professional person who didn't really care about their job and their customer. There is no substitute for honest concern and a commitment to deliver the best you have to offer, remember the customer is you and me! Can't you always tell when someone honestly cares about the level of service they are giving you?

I know that we have talked about many concepts throughout this book. I also know that, probably much like me, you will remember some and forget some. You will probably, at one point or another, say to yourself...

"What did he say about...?"

So, on the next page I have put together a Quick Reference Guide that will help to jog your memory in case you don't have the time to re-read this whole book.

Quick Reference Guide
Aiming For Excellence

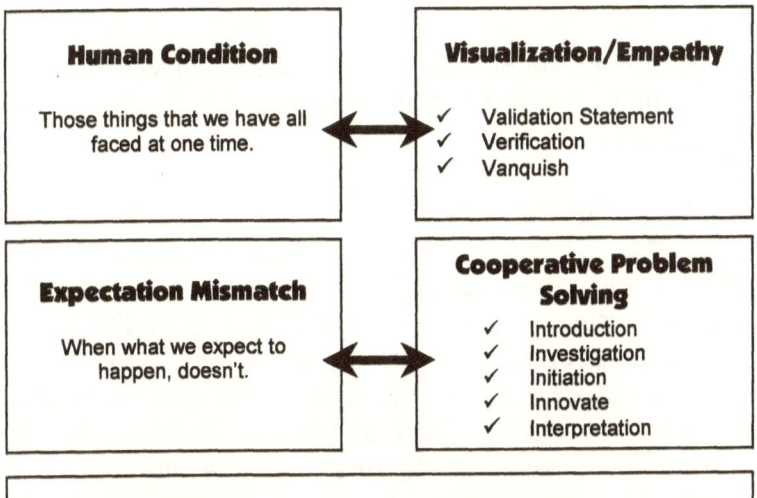

Human Condition	**Visualization/Empathy**
Those things that we have all faced at one time.	✓ Validation Statement ✓ Verification ✓ Vanquish

Expectation Mismatch	**Cooperative Problem Solving**
When what we expect to happen, doesn't.	✓ Introduction ✓ Investigation ✓ Initiation ✓ Innovate ✓ Interpretation

Customer Types

Customer Types	Techniques
Junkyard Dog	Cooperative Problem Solving
Squirrels	Cooperative Problem Solving
Bunnies	Visualization/Empathy
Donkeys	Visualization/Empathy
Peacocks	Visualization/Empathy

Opportunities for Excellence	**Everyday Extraordinary Service**
Ways to exceed the customers expectations. Capitalize on every opportunity presented.	Observation *of the Customer's needs* Reaction *to the Customer's needs*

Four Aspects of Professionalism

✓ Attentive
✓ Interactive
✓ Poised
✓ Committed

Random Thoughts

What is Excellent Customer Service?

Here is one of the shortest definitions I can think of, it is, quite simply, *having a positive, personal relationship with your customer(s)!*

Too Many Customers...

I remember some of my first customer service moments. I was 16 and I had just gotten a job at a brand new fast food restaurant. I was overwhelmed with the sheer number of people who came in. When I was being utilized as a cashier it was a little intimidating seeing what seemed like a hundred people in line. Then I realized that I was too focused on the big picture (a good trait for the manager but not for an inexperienced cashier). It came to me very clearly one magical moment. *"There is no other customer, other than the one I am waiting on right now."* That mini-revelation suddenly put everything into perspective for me and also allowed me to focus on the needs of that one person. My nervousness vanished and my customer service skills increased 10 fold just by changing my perspective that very little bit.

You Can't Win Them All...

This goes way back to those first pages you read. I told you I would be honest with you. Sometimes despite our very best efforts we are going to fail to please a customer. As long as it is not from lack of effort or skill then you have to "let it go". There are some folks who refuse to be satisfied but guess what? There is a silver lining even to those situations!

First, these are the customers who really test your skills and thereby force you to try harder than you ever have before. Secondly, there are probably others watching you and your efforts will not be lost on them.

Whether they are other customers or even fellow workers someone else is appreciating your efforts. In fact there will always be at least one other person who will be thrilled by your efforts, ME!! So if you have to …pretend that I am standing there with you when you get into one of these situations…who knows it just might help.

Develop Your Own Personal Customer Service Style…
While it is very nice that you are reading my thoughts and practicing some of my suggestions you also need to develop a style that is comfortable to you. If you can take some of these techniques and blend them, incorporate them into your own customer service arsenal you will truly become a force to be reckoned with in the customer service arena.

Well…that is it my friends!
Congratulations and Thank You!

Let me remind you of the commitment you made in the beginning of this book namely, that you will:

✓ Consider the ideas presented here.
✓ Try at least one of these techniques.
✓ Speak with someone about your thoughts and insights to Customer Service after having read this book.

I appreciate your time, your level of commitment and your desire to excel at customer service. I hope I have given you some assistance in attaining that very worthwhile goal!

Please feel free to contact me with any comments, suggestions or insights you might have and remember to discuss this topic with at least one other person!

The discussion you have will, no doubt, be helpful too. All the best…

Keep Aiming for Excellence!

Sincerely
Tim Bonomo

68